My Life in Fortune Cookies

Dimitra Merkouris

Ten|16
PRESS

www.ten16press.com - Waukesha, WI

For information, please contact:

Ten│16
PRESS

www.ten16press.com
Waukesha, WI

Edited by Jenna Zerbel
Cover design by Jayden Shambeau
Art direction by Kaeley Dunteman

if god gave you an orange first appeared in *Last Leaves Magazine* issue 2

Advanced Praise for
My Life in Fortune Cookies

"With an eclectic style that favours truth bathed in hard, sweet imagery over poetic whimsy and cliché, Dimitra Merkouris delivers a poke in the eye of contemporary suburban ennui with musings on regret, parenthood, careerism and the collective consciousness of first-generation immigrants. Merkouris dedicated her new poetry collection to her sisters, but she gifted it to all of us."

—Joel Ceausu, Journalist/Reporter at
The Suburban Newspaper

"Dimitra Merkouris' *My Life in Fortune Cookies* is a beautiful expansion on her form, style, and views of the world. From her personal experiences to larger commentaries on misogyny and immigration, Dimitra finds moments in yellow finches and Sunday morning smells to create a collection that will make you feel like your footsteps are falling alongside hers. *My Life in Fortune Cookies* will have you walking beside Dimitra, living, smelling, and feeling what surrounds her."

—Editors of *Last Leaves Magazine*

"*My Life in Fortune Cookies* by Dimitra Merkouris is a debut poetry collection that makes you want to read over the same poem once you're done. The imagery and narratives evoke a longing for the past and a wanting of the future. Merkouris' crisp words and flowing metaphors keep you captivated with every flip of the page. You will feel uncomfortable, vulnerable, but most importantly, you will feel alive while reading *My Life in Fortune Cookies*. There is one thing for sure—you will feel it all, as the words come crashing into your soul."

—Christina Strigas, author of *Love & Metaxa*

For my sisters,
Kathy and Ria

A Tiny Verse for Our Tiny Villain

Beware Covid. A chaos-king.
Unfettered fiend to friend and foe.
Caustic creep, airborne-thief—an
Invisible, insidious, evil interloper.

Misogyny in the Workplace

To live a life without self-reflection,
Is to live half-masted.
Drifting, drifting, drifting,
Through the unexamined soul—

> Why is the misogyny in an operating room theatre
> a far scarier incidental event than the postpartum
> hemorrhage saturating the Teflon scrubs of a surgeon
> with his hands clamped down inside a uterus that
> refuses to contract? How is it best to divert the
> avalanche of blood and afterbirth to a trickle? One
> that slowly meanders its way down the stainless steel
> table and onto the floor.

Or is it truly best to stay the course,
Lost in the language of translation.
Safety first.

Truth Bomb Shelter

Beware the gaslighter!
She'll sell you down the river for two hundred and forty-five dollars
Or fifty micrograms of
Today's special
All the while cowering behind her shields of conformity,
In a vacuum-like existence—
Sucking up all the oxygen in the atmosphere.
"It's only milf weed," she purrs, batting her pale eyelashes.
"Nutrient-rich like new mother's milk.
The kind you just happen across...accidentally..."
(Hidden in plain sight as if it's no big deal).
"Sprinkle it delicately over
Perfectly portioned suburban salads like
Triple-washed, prepackaged devil's lettuce,"
She simpers coquettishly.
"Roll it up and cram it inside your kid's moldy,
Grass-stained, striped athletic tube sock."

Dear Aunt Lydia,
Thank you for your words of wisdom, however,
I wasn't born yesterday, although I was borne of yesterday.
What you're talking about isn't a pretty pink pill
that dissolves sweetly under one's tongue.

What you're talking about is the straight up kind. Potent.
Undiluted. Unmasked.
The numbing kind that promises oblivion,
Or absolution, or salvation,
Or whatever gets you through the day.
Can you hear the church bells ringing? I can.
I have no need of your cattle prod.
I've reached my fill of hand wringing.
I just can't listen to your version of events any longer.
I can't light the oil lamp that casts shadows over your bloated face.
I can't hold back your yellow strawed acrid hair as you retch,
Turning yourself inside out
Asking me to light the match
That will engulf us both in flames.
I refuse to be consumed by you.
In the dead of the night when sleep evades us both,
We both know you're nowhere near as all-encompassing
As you pretend to be,
Nowhere near the power of my spoken truth.

The Immigrant Song

(My mother and your mother were washing the clothes)

The girl stands, plucking branches in the wide expanse of the olive grove. Gazing upwards, she closes her eyes to the heavens and welcomes the unexpected breeze dancing through her hair. It cools her sweat-drenched brow and the nape of her neck. The girl knows that the wind wants to trick her, that it leaves behind a salty residue that no amount of scrubbing can erase. Soon her once sun-kissed coppery tresses will be gone forever. The girl knows this, and still she welcomes the brief respite from a hellish day. Suddenly the wind rises, making the ruffles of her newly gifted dress snap westward across her chest like a flag lying at half-mast across her milk-heavy bosom—testing her resolve and playing games not meant for the weak of heart. Dust swirls at her feet. She's barefoot. The girl looks down at the ebony fabric of her mourning gown and thinks of how it was so hastily sewn together by the same brown-spotted and slightly gnarled fingers that reached into her very core and pulled into the world the mewling cries of all her hungry children. She did remember to say thank you.

(My mother gave your mother a punch in the nose)

The girl stands, stretching up onto her toes with arms outstretched and reaching up to the heavens, straightening out the kinks that seem to have taken up permanent residence in her spine. She does this whilst standing in the cavernous belly of a stainless steel beast, listening to the whir of clicking needles—a perfectly synchronized song of a thousand nightingales masking the creaking of aching and porous bones and the back-and-forth roll of a rocking chair that's been purposefully nailed to the floor. The girl thinks how nice it would have been if their porthole had been left slightly ajar. Squinting up at harsh fluorescent lights, the girl turns racoon eyes back to plucking errant threads off of cashmere sweaters and musing over the sound of stamps on passports. The punch of 4x6 rectangles bears the ink-smudged letters of her name.

(What color was the blood)

The woman sits hunched over needlework. With every surface of her two-bedroom apartment properly encapsulated by intricately woven doilies in every shade of cream known to man, the woman can finally turn her hands to knitting capes. Capes for her many granddaughters to wear over red ruffled dresses, white knee-high socks, and black Mary Janes polished to a high gloss. The woman hopes that one day, when her granddaughters look down—bored while queued up near the nave of the church, mouths slightly agape and restless in their readiness to receive their Holy Communion—they just might catch a glimpse of the girl as she once was: standing in the shadow of a giant fleur-de-lis, clutching a maple leaf to her heart, and singing a litany of just what it takes to run headlong into the winds of change.

My Little Yellow Finch

I see my little yellow finch,
sitting on a wire—jerking
her head left and twitching
her neck right. As my heart skips a beat,
as my breath catches in my throat, I see
my little yellow finch, claiming this day,
this hour, this very moment, to
launch herself decidedly into the air.

She rides headlong into the day's gentle current.
I resist temptation of calling out,
my lips forming warnings of my own trepidation.
I hear the echoes of all my sisters before me. They whisper,
"Watch. Wait. It's time to let go. She's got this."
It's true. Her small, perfectly formed wings are made for flight.
I am left behind, watching her tiny form undulate before me,
picking up speed and embracing the warmth
of an early summer morning.

Breathless, I am spellbound,
watching the rising and falling of
this sunshine sweetened gumdrop soaring before my eyes.

I am greedy. I gulp. I understand.
I inhale, trying to extract more than my allotted
twenty-one percent.
I am grounded, relegated to spectator status. Still
I watch, buttercup wings and sunflower feathers cascading like
waterfalls of liquid gold.

This thick cascade of warm honey is, quite frankly,
sweetness personified. I take.
I drink my fill. I fill my cup. My cup spills over.
My little yellow finch decides
to alight herself (somewhat dizzily) on
one of the lowest hanging branches of our
forty-year-old maple tree.
She proudly begins preening her windswept feathers,
completely oblivious to me.

She warbles her delight. Her song rises into the air.
Hearing this happy trilling,
this selfless birdsong,
fills us both with élan, with wonder,
and finally, I can let go.
I hold my breast, my heart, and
slowly, slowly, slowly,
I exhale.

Mother of the Year

Click clack click clack
NHL quality slap shot precision.
Pushing a shopping cart piled high with juice boxes, bread,
and four different kinds of apples.
She careens around corners in sensible one-inch pumps worn
because they just happen to be,
absolutely perfect,
for squashing those pesky black beetles one might find
scurrying across the driveway.
The ones that make her beige-lined lips purse into subtle
(almost imperceptible) pouts of distaste,
because, after all, she's just trying to get into her Audi to
produce
produce
produce.
Those pesky black beetles are
reminders of warm summers, and
she's forced to pause, listen
to the sound of rustling leaves, even
the ones at the very top of blooming birch trees.
These landscapes are best left in pictures
hanging in waiting rooms.

It's hard to talk about Caribbean cruises where the sun is shining,
instead of forty below zero.
Even the dead can hear those whispers in the wind.
Reminder: pick up bug spray.

Click clack click clack
NHL quality slap shot precision.
She marches into teacher lounges (deserted now) as
the sun sets over the freshly poured concrete of the parking lot,
clutching her binder stuffed with spreadsheets,
lists,
selfless good intentions,
like a Girl Scout yearning for her badge.
She stares, glassy-eyed, at a spot on the wall precisely
eight centimeters above the perfect ponytail of
a Lululemon wearing,
cupcake baking,
rainbow making,
former this or former that.
Yawn. Sigh. Stretch. Arms extend way over head,
almost touch the sky.
Pass me the conch.
"We're all here for the children," repeats on a loop.

"Piggy,
p-i-g-g-y,
PIGGY!"
Click clack click clack
NHL quality snapshot precision.
Click, click, click

> Warning: Strobe lighting has been known to cause
> permanent blindness! Staggering into balloon
> festooned rooms, whispers don't cause an echo, careful
> not to bump into each other because it's their first
> time in heels—hopefully kitten heels and tugging at
> neckties tied just a smidgen too tight.

Ahem...
There's nothing wrong with yellow pantsuits,
Dairy Queen, and
two scoops of mint chocolate chip on a sugar cone.
The stench of gymnasiums is
the acrid perfume of my childhood.
We're all here for the children. And yet,
it's important to clutch a dozen red roses tightly to one's chest
as you strut across the stage,
lest you drop one.
"Don't slip on the sequins littering the floor, Karen."
Mother of the Year.

Pigtails, Pinafores, and Pumps

I can remember
Sitting in the auditorium listening to the MAN speak about life
The road less traveled
Opportunity
And choice
I can still feel humming in my chest
The vibrations of a train approaching the station
The wind caressing the loose tendrils of my hair
Picking up speed
The sound thundering in my ears
Whipping my hair in every direction until at last
My tightly woven plaits hang free
And as the frenzy subsides
I see two ribbons
Lying at my feet

I can remember
Thinking of the sound curtains make
As they swish together over the stage
Like an owl swooping through midnight's embrace
A mouse's tail dangling limply in its tightly clenched talons
A veritable feast

Looking down I can still see one perfectly formed drop of blood
Staining the front of my crisp white button-down Oxford shirt
Dreams lying like collateral damage on the side of a highway
Perfectly camouflageable by the ruffles of my pinafore
The weight of expectations worn with a wink and a smile
And a thank you ma'am
Let's talk about glass ceilings
And butterfly wings beating against mason jars

I can remember
Seeing multihued stars exploding like
Disney fireworks from behind
Rubbing the sleep out of the corners of my eyes
Using the palms of my hand
None too gently
The absolute shock of midday sun on alabaster skin
Blindingly
Illuminatingly
Reflectively
A colt with legs splayed out beneath it
In four different directions
Numbness
Its expiration date is long past
I take a deep breath
Thank you transplant surgeon

Did you know the DOCTOR blew up
The lungs of the very lovely lady
Who signed her card in exactly the right place
Before stapling them shut?
Now I can go on my way to the honey tree
Long legs striding along confidently
A barely perceptible shock of crimson peeking out
From the underside of my brand-new shoes
The hot sun at my back
I look down
See how I tower over the shadow lying in front of me
Do you see the barely perceptible yellow chalk outline
Tracing the contours of my distorted form
I see it
No matter which way I turn
No matter the rain
Like when my daughter thought it would be a good idea
To use permanent marker to play
Connect the dots on her bedroom wall
And tried to wash it away before I could see it
Such a lovely pattern
No matter
I jump
Clicking my heels together
Finding my way home.

I See You

I see you
Lying on your bedroom floor in a patch of sunlight
Tracing swirls and whorls into the carpet
Cushioning the lithe contours of your body
Over and over and over again
Listening to the sizzle of diced onions and minced garlic
The heady aroma of my Sunday mornings
Making your nose wrinkle ever so slightly

I see you
Sitting at the kitchen table
Tapping your fork against the side of a heavily laden dinner plate
Waiting for a pause
The incessant droning of bees encompassing your head
Piercing your meat like a fisherman spear
Diving into warm tropical waters
The meat so tender it falls off the bone
Rolling your eyes

I see you
Standing on the porch while the rain hammers down
Nails pounding into the asphalt
The pleats of your tartan kilt razor sharp and bone dry
Clutching a phone to your heart
While I hold a Costco umbrella over your head

I see you
Running towards the yellow ribbon strung across the finish line
Oblivious to everything
Except the neon pink stripe
Bouncing at the outermost edge of your tunnel vision
Gasping for air
The sound of my cheers falling on deaf ears

I see you
Flying through the air
Laughing and swinging this warm summer evening
Like we used to play in dawn's early light
Although it sometimes feels like an eternity
I know it won't last
I know it doesn't matter
All that matters—
I see you.

Walking Amongst Time

Walking amongst friends
Eyes recounting jokes not yet spoken
In a throng of backpacks
There was one
Only one
With a bag slung casually across his chest
Across his heart
I leaned back in my chair
Red lips smiling
Feet tapping
Simply unaware.

   Walking amongst trees
   Ears filled with birdsong
   There were two, only two
   Sets of footprints on the earth
   The hard earth
   Pine needles cushioned our steps
   Woodsmoke filled our lungs.

Walking amongst sheep
Heads hung low
The weight of burdens not yet lifted
Waiting to be lifted, carried
Always waiting
An insurmountable feat.

Walking amongst waves
Ankle deep
Knee deep
Over our heads
We jump out laughing
Salt stinging my eyes and the tiny razor cuts on my legs
Your face
Unnoticed
A buoy bobs in the distance
I turn and stare at the tiny hand grasping mine
Red lips turn to blue
Nothing else matters

It's time to go
I know now what to do
My eyes recount jokes not yet spoken
You smile.

Bluebirds in Spring

Flying

Soaring

Swooping

Trilling their delight

How my heart fills with hope

Whenever bluebirds alight

To serenade me through my window

With their sweet, sweet song

Waking me from my slumber

That is winter's endless night.

if god gave you an orange

if god gave you an orange
would you reach out your hands
fingers splayed
grasping
gasping and
biting
into its sweetness

knowing that
explosions of juice
would spray your face
trickle
down
your
chin and
settle
into the deep crevices
of your chest

a perfectly divine
stickiness
extracted
from

sun-warmed and
heavy-hanging fruit

echoing the hum
of half-drunk
bumblebees

drowsily,
mind-numbingly
random

intent
on pollinating
the whole
wide
world

or

would you give
the impression
of rapt attention while
dangling that
damned
orange

against your earlobe
scoping out
reasons
to complain
about
natural sugars
versus artificial sweeteners

that left you with the world's
most
bittersweet
aftertaste

I think you will always find
reasons to
complain,
even
if the aftertaste
left
in
your
mouth
was laced with
honeyed
sunshine.

The World is Not Your Oyster

The world is not your oyster
Rose-tinted glasses are a luxury
The world is equal parts beauty and horror
An endeavor not meant for the weak of heart
Each morning is an exercise in determination
Resilience
And hope.
And seeing as we all have moments of weakness
Of darkness
And chaos,
Surround yourself with the people who will hold you up
Against time and space and this very moment.
It's called faith
And maybe, just maybe,
Collectively
It's possible to find some measure of peace
Acceptance
The will to go on
Perhaps it's all an exercise in futility
Bathed in a simpleton's delight
With beautiful optimism
Platitudes aplenty

A gravedigger's bread and butter
Adding weight to a collection basket
Passed around from person to person
Hand to hand
Mouth to mouth
Until the buck stops with you.

General Anesthesia

I had no idea
When I married you
I was marrying the establishment.

> I was too young and naive
> To care much about all-wheel drive,
> Monogrammed dress shirts, and matching cuff links.

Utterly brainwashed as I was by the sterility of my very existence,
Your strange urges to whitewash our picket fence,
And cut the grass with an old pair of scissors.

> My mother raised me to
> Learn the meaning of words
> Like homeostasis. Induction. Minimum alveolar concentration.
> All they got me was knee-deep in piss and shit.
> Blood and guts.
> A paycheck every other Thursday.
> The smell of burning flesh, fat, and fun
> I saw, from my bird's eye view of a room,
> Hell-bent on keeping a stranger alive,
> That I was slowly dying inside.

Sometimes, when I stuck my head inside your mouth,
Pretending to admire an unobstructed view
Of your glistening vocal cords,
Paralyzed to the hilt, I would appreciate the rings of your trachea,
The narrative they spoke to me,
And the lion's roar in my head would stay a faraway echo.
I could forget about what it costs,
To ram my breathing tube down your throat.

Oprah asked me afterwards,
"Were you silent or were you silenced?"
Neither. Both.
"Be a lady," they said.

Gently now. I wouldn't want to damage any teeth.
Hurry now. It's not my fault you nicked the artery.
Hemorrhage, hemorrhage, hemorrhage
All over the floor.
Cortisol fueling breakfast, lunch, and dinner.
While propofol never lasts.
Eyes twitching. Teeth grinding. Middle of the night ringing.
A long series of fifteen-minute union breaks.
Just enough time to find
Colleagues lying on the bathroom floor or
Colleagues courting in the on-call room.

Pupils constricting. Pupils dilating. Shining my light.
The whole world falling apart, the whole world starting over.
Shining my light. Shine, baby, shine.

I'm the mother now.
There are no end stops.
It doesn't have to be a circus.
All of life is a series of poetic verse written in enjambment
Waiting for me to pick up a pen
And start writing.

You told me, many years later,
In the peaceful silence that comes in the aftermath of a heavy row,
Everything you learned about the counterculture revolution.

Watching me out of the corner of your eye
As I discovered myself
The day I gave the finger to the MAN one random Tuesday.

I learned too. You see, in the end it ain't so bad,
To drive a Volvo. Sip a latte. Schmooze the husband's boss.
Maybe I'm part establishment too.

The Twelfth Month

Snow falls softly through December's sweet mornings,
shrouding a sentimental empiricism
based on logic and reasoning, an anemic
vanishing in the pale and weak light.

Leaving exposed raw and gaping wounds
of a life lived fully, and scars are
tattooed accounts of the machinations
of the body's vast highway of blood.
Words whispered only under the cover of a deep darkness.

The hours when souls are laid bare with
impromptu confessionals that travel through the air,
lest the sound of scratching at the door is
indeed, more than my gentleman caller.

What is life when filled with moments made meaningless
by manufactured self-importance?
The pastoral harmony of bees is truly a balm
to better buzz my humanist soul to sleep.